T0322844

World premiere

THE RETURN OF
BENJAMIN LAY

by
Naomi Wallace and Marcus Rediker

FINBOROUGH
THEATRE

First performance at the Finborough Theatre: Tuesday, 13 June 2023

THE RETURN OF BENJAMIN LAY

by Naomi Wallace and Marcus Rediker

Cast

Benjamin Lay   **Mark Povinelli**

2023. A Quaker meeting house – or is it a theatre?

Director	**Ron Daniels**
Set Designers	**Riccardo Hernandez** and **Isobel Nicolson**
Costume Designer	**Isobel Nicolson**
Lighting Designer	**Anthony Doran**
Sound Designer	**John Leonard**
Movement Consultant	**Bill Irwin**
Stage Manager	**Martha J. Baldwin**
Producer	**Arsalan Sattari**

The approximate running time is 75 minutes.

There will be no interval.

Mark Povinelli | Benjamin Lay

Mark is most known for his critically acclaimed performance as Torvald Helmer in the OBIE award winning production of *Mabou Mines DollHouse* (St. Ann's Warehouse and International Tour) as well as the premiere of Martha Clarke's *Belle Epoque* (Lincoln Center) in the lead role of Henri Toulouse-Lautrec. Other theatre includes performances at the Shakespeare Theater, Children's Theater Company, Radio City Music Hall, Oklahoma Lyric Theater, Will Geer Theatricum and UCLA Live.

Film includes *Nightmare Alley, Water For Elephants, Mirror Mirror, The Hot Flashes* and *My Dinner With Hervé*.

Television includes *Modern Family, Criminal Minds, Happyish, Boardwalk Empire, Charmed* and *Mad Dogs*.

Mark became the first little person cast as a series regular on a network sitcom in *Are You There, Chelsea?*

As a noted social activist, in June 2017, Povinelli was elected President of the Little People of America which promotes awareness, advocacy and medical assistance for individuals with forms of dwarfism.

Naomi Wallace | Playwright

Naomi Wallace returns to the Finborough Theatre which saw the production of her first play, *The War Plays*, and more recently an acclaimed adaptation of *Returning to Haifa* by Ghassan Kanafani, co-written with Ismail Khalidi. Her plays have been produced in the UK, the United States, Europe and the Middle East and include *One Flea Spare, The Breach, The Trestle at Pope Lick Creek, In the Heart of America, Slaughter City, Things of Dry Hours, The Fever Chart: Three Vision of the Middle East, And I and Silence, The Liquid Plain, Night is a Room* and two adaptations co-written with Ismail Khalidi, *Returning to Haifa* by Ghassan Kanafani and *The Corpse Washer* by Sinan Antoon. Awards include the MacArthur Award, Obie Award, Susan Smith Blackburn Prize, Fellowship of Southern Writers Drama Award, Horton Foote Award, Arts and Letters Award in Literature, and the inaugural Windham Campbell prize for drama. Wallace is currently writing the book for the new John Mellencamp musical *Small Town*. The second part of her Kentucky trilogy will be produced in France in 2024, and her play, *Night is a Room*, has been adapted for film and will star Ann Dowd.

Marcus Rediker | Playwright and Historian

Writer and historian Marcus Rediker is Distinguished Professor of Atlantic History at the University of Pittsburgh. His "histories from below," including *The Slave Ship: A Human History*, have won numerous awards, including the George Washington Book Prize, and have been translated into eighteen languages worldwide. He is the author of *The Fearless Benjamin Lay: The Quaker Dwarf Who Became the First Revolutionary Abolitionist*, co-author (with David Lester and Paul Buhle) of *Prophet against Slavery: Benjamin Lay, A Graphic Novel,* and producer of a prize-winning documentary film, *Ghosts of Amistad*, directed by Tony Buba. He worked with Naomi Wallace on her play *The Liquid Plain*. He is currently writing a book about escaping slavery by sea in antebellum America.

Ron Daniels | Director

Ron Daniels was named Honorary Associate Director after fifteen years directing many productions for the Royal Shakespeare Company including *Hamlet* (with Mark Rylance and another with Roger Rees), *The Tempest* (with Derek Jacobi and Mark Rylance) as well as new plays by Stephen Poliakoff, David Rudkin, Pam Gems and David Edgar, including Naomi Wallace's *Slaughter City* and Anthony Burgess' *A Clockwork Orange*.

Ron is a former Associate Artistic Director of the American Repertory Theatre where he directed productions including *Henry IV Parts 1 and 2*, *Henry V*, *The Tempest*, *The Cherry Orchard*, *Hamlet*, and *The Seagull* with Mark Rylance. Other theatres include *Othello* (Shakespeare Theatre, Washington DC), *Richard II*, *Richard III* and *Macbeth* (Theatre for a New Audience), Naomi Wallace's *One Flea Spare* (Public Theater, New York City), *Much Ado about Nothing* and *The Taming of the Shrew* (Old Globe, San Diego).

Opera includes *Madama Butterfly*, *La Bohème*, *Carmen*, and *Don Giovanni*, the world premiere productions of Daniel Catan's *Il Postino* with Placido Domingo, Ricky Ian Gordon's *Morning Star* and Daniel Schnyder's *Charlie Parker's Yardbird*.

Film includes Naomi Wallace and Bruce McLeod's *Lawn Dogs* (Executive Producer) and *The War Boys*.

He is a former head of the Institute for Advanced Theatre Training at Harvard University, where he taught acting and directing.

Riccardo Hernandez | Set Designer

Riccardo's numerous productions include *Jagged Little Pill* (Tony Nomination for Best Scenic Design of a Musical), *Frankie and Johnny in the Clair de Lune* (Tony Nomination for Best Revival of a Play) starring Audra McDonald and Michael Shannon, *Indecent* (2017 Tony Award Best Play Nomination – Broadway and Menier Chocolate Factory, London), *The Gin Game* with James Earl Jones and Cicely Tyson, *Porgy and Bess* (2012 Tony Award Best Musical Revival), *The People in the Picture* (Studio 54), *Caroline, or Change* (2007 Olivier Award for Best New Musical and *London Evening Standard* Award for Best Musical 2006), *TopDog/UnderDog* (2002 Pulitzer Award Best Play – Broadway and Royal Court Theatre, London) and *Parade* (Tony Award and Drama Desk Nominations).

Riccardo has designed over 250 productions at most leading Regional Theatres and Operas across the US and internationally, over twenty productions at the American Rep Theatre, and over thirty productions at New York Shakespeare Festival and Public Theater.

Awards and Nominations include Obie Award Sustained Excellence of Scenic Design, Henry Hewes Design Award Outstanding Scenic Design, Princess Grace Statue Award, Princess Grace Grant, Drama Desk Awards, Connecticut Critics Circle, Helen Hayes Award, Audelco, American Theater Wing and the Boston Elliot Norton Award.

He is the Associate Professor of Theater Design at Yale School of Drama.

Isobel Nicolson | Set and Costume Designer

Isobel is a Creative Associate at the Watermill Theatre, Newbury. She was a Resident Assistant Designer with the Royal Shakespeare Company 2019-2020.

Theatre includes *Rapunzel, Camp Albion, A Christmas Carol, Moonfleet, Digging for Victory, The Miller's Child* (Watermill Theatre, Newbury), *Lone Flyer* (Hull Truck Theatre, Jermyn Street Theatre and the Watermill Theatre, Newbury), *Jessie's Tattoo Club* (Bristol Old Vic Ferment), *Queen Mab* (Iris Theatre), *Jabberwocky* (The Other Palace and Theatre Royal Margate), *Tis Pity She's A Whore* (Sherman Studio, Cardiff), *Dream* (The Other Place and The New Vic Theatre, Staffordshire), *Errol's Garden* (UK tour), *Old Friends* (Cambridge Junction and the Cockpit Theatre), *D-Day75* (101 Outdoor Arts), *The Witches* (Watford Palace Theatre), *Die Fledermaus* (DEPOT and Spit & Sawdust Skatepark) and *Bright Young Things* and *Stay Brave Brian Gravy* (Theatre Royal Bury St Edmunds).

Associate Designs include *My Neighbour Totoro* (Royal Shakespeare Company at the Barbican Theatre), *Island Nation* (Arcola Theatre), *The Velveteen Rabbit* and *The Old Curiosity Shop* (UK tour).

Anthony Doran | Lighting Designer

Anthony returns to the Finborough Theatre following the critically acclaimed *Scrounger* for which he was nominated for an OffWestEnd Award.

He is an acclaimed designer for numerous productions in the UK, New York and Europe. Theatre includes *The Cherry Orchard, Bluets* (Deutsches Schauspielhaus, Hamburg), *In Real Life, Schatten* and *Orlando* (Schaubühne), *Killing It* (Network theatre, Vaults Festival), *Norma Jean Baker of Troy* (Kenneth C. Griffin Theatre, The Shed New York), *La Maladie de laMort* (Théâtre des Bouffes du Nord, Paris), *A Colder Water* (Vaults Festival) and *Asymptote* (Laban).

Associate Lighting Designs include *Greatest Play* (Trafalgar Theatre) and *Kuala Khan* (Oily Cart).

John Leonard | Sound Designer

John started work as a sound designer before the term was even coined in the UK. He was Head of Sound at the Royal Shakespeare Company and an Associate Artist, and has worked for most of the major theatre companies in the UK, including the National Theatre, the English National Opera, Hampstead Theatre, Almeida Theatre, Donmar Warehouse and extensively in London's West End, Broadway and on national and international tours.

Recent theatre includes *4000 Miles* (Chichester Minerva Theatre), *As You Like It* (Soho Place Theatre), *The Sex Party* (Menier Chocolate Factory), *The Snail House, Night Mother, Wolf Cub, Cell Mates, The Meeting, Stevie* (Hampstead Theatre), *The Dresser* (Theatre Royal Bath and UK tour), *The Stepmother, 8 Hotels* (Minerva Theatre, Chichester), *Prism* (Hampstead Theatre and UK tour), *Blithe Spirit* (Theatre Royal Bath, UK Tour and West End), *Consent, Cocktail Sticks* (National Theatre and West End), *My Name Is Lucy Barton* (Bridge Theatre and Friedman Theatre, New York City), *Uncle Vanya* (Theatre Royal Bath), *Charlotte & Theodore, In Praise Of Love* (Ustinov Theatre, Bath), *Long Day's Journey Into Night* (Bristol Old Vic, West End, New York and Los Angeles), *Hand To God* (Vaudeville

Theatre), *McQueen* (St. James Theatre and West End), *Firebird, Mr. Foote's Other Leg* (Hampstead Theatre and West End), *Ghosts* (Almeida Theatre, West End and Harvey Theatre, Brooklyn).

Exhibitions include those for The Tussauds Group in London, Warwick Castle, Amsterdam and New York,

He is the author of a renowned textbook on theatre sound, winner of Drama Desk and Sound Designer of The Year Awards and is a Fellow of the Guildhall School of Music and Drama, an Honorary Fellow of The Hong Kong Academy of Performing Arts and a Companion of the Liverpool Institute of Performing Arts.

Bill Irwin | Movement Consultant

Bill is an American actor, clown and comedian. He began as a vaudeville-style stage performer and has been noted for his contribution to the renaissance of American circus during the 1970s. He has made a number of appearances on film and television, and won a Tony Award for his role in *Who's Afraid of Virginia Woolf?* on Broadway.

Irwin was awarded the National Endowment for the Arts Choreographer's Fellowship in 1981 and 1983. In 1984, he was named a Guggenheim Fellow and was the first performance artist to be awarded a five-year MacArthur Fellowship. For *Largely New York* (five Tony Award nominations), he won a New York Drama Critics Circle Special Citation in 1988 and an Outer Critics Circle Award and Drama Desk Award in 1989.

Production Acknowledgements

Press Relations	**Chloé Nelkin Consulting**
Set Builder	**Alex Marker**
Costume Makers	**Louise Jane Patey**
	Chris White
	Antique House Crafts
	Novis Shoes
Extra Sound Equipment	**Autograph Sound Recording**
Artwork Design	**Arsalan Sattari**

Special thanks to the Irish Repertory Theatre in New York, Emily Barratt, Eleanor Hicks, Rob Nagle, Seb Noel; Heather, Keaton and Piper Povinelli; and Kathleen Blee, Bettye J. and Ralph E. Bailey Dean of Kenneth P. Dietrich School of Arts and Sciences, University of Pittsburgh.

The playwrights would like to thank Mark Brokaw, Ben Goffe, Matthew Jeffers, Raz Shaw and the New York Theater Workshop and Signature Theater in New York; and Guy Delamarche, Dominique Hollier, René Loyon and Théâtre du Lucernaire in Paris, for their help in the development of this play. Special thanks to Andrew Haggas for his wisdom about sheep.

Thanks to Loretta Fox, Dave Wermeling, Rosie Bothwell, Avis Wanda McClinton, and Tim Gee for helping their own Quaker communities in the US and the UK to re-embrace Benjamin Lay.

The producers would like to thank Tom Brocklehurst, Stella Kanu and Kris Nelson at LIFT for enabling us to bring international theatre talent to the UK.

This production is proudly supported by the **University of Pittsburgh**.

FINBOROUGH THEATRE

© Alan Cox

'Probably the most influential fringe theatre in the world.' *Time Out*

'Not just a theatre, but a miracle.' *Metro*

'The mighty little Finborough which, under Neil McPherson, continues to offer a mixture of neglected classics and new writing in a cannily curated mix.' Lyn Gardner, *The Stage*

'The tiny but mighty Finborough.' Ben Brantley, *The New York Times*

Founded in 1980, the multi-award-winning Finborough Theatre presents plays and music theatre, concentrated exclusively on vibrant new writing and unique rediscoveries – both in our 155 year old home and online with our new digital initiative – #FinboroughFrontier

Our programme is unique – we never present work that has been seen anywhere in London during the last 25 years. Behind the scenes, we continue to discover and develop a new generation of theatre makers. Despite remaining completely unsubsidised, the Finborough Theatre has an unparalleled track record for attracting the finest talent who go on to become leading voices in British theatre. Under Artistic Director Neil McPherson, it has discovered some of the UK's most exciting new playwrights including Laura Wade, James Graham, Mike Bartlett, Jack Thorne, Carmen Nasr, Athena Stevens and Anders Lustgarten, and directors including Tamara Harvey, Robert Hastie, Blanche McIntyre, Kate Wasserberg and Sam Yates.

Artists working at the theatre in the 1980s included Clive Barker, Rory Bremner, Nica Burns, Kathy Burke, Ken Campbell, Jane Horrocks, Nicola Walker and Claire Dowie. In the 1990s, the Finborough Theatre first became known for new writing including Naomi Wallace's first play *The War Boys*, Rachel Weisz in David Farr's *Neville Southall's Washbag*, four plays by Anthony Neilson including *Penetrator* and *The Censor*, both of which transferred to the Royal Court Theatre, and new plays by Richard Bean, Lucinda Coxon, David Eldridge and Tony Marchant. New writing development included the premieres of modern classics such as Mark Ravenhill's *Shopping and F***king*, Conor McPherson's *This Lime Tree Bower*, Naomi Wallace's *Slaughter City* and Martin McDonagh's *The Pillowman*.

Since 2000, new British plays have included Laura Wade's London debut *Young Emma*, commissioned for the Finborough Theatre, James Graham's London debut *Albert's Boy* with Victor Spinetti, Sarah Grochala's *S27*, Athena Stevens' *Schism* which was nominated for an Olivier Award, and West End transfers for Joy Wilkinson's *Fair*, Nicholas de Jongh's *Plague Over England*, Jack Thorne's *Fanny and Faggot*, Neil McPherson's Olivier Award nominated *It Is Easy To Be Dead*, and Dawn King's *Foxfinder*.

UK premieres of foreign plays have included plays by Lanford Wilson, Larry Kramer, Tennessee Williams, Suzan-Lori Parks, the English premieres of two Scots language classics by Robert McLellan, and more Canadian plays than any other theatre in Europe, with West End transfers for Frank McGuinness' *Gates of Gold* with William Gaunt, and Craig Higginson's *Dream of the Dog* with Dame Janet Suzman. In December 2022, the Finborough Theatre became the first foreign theatre to perform in Ukraine since the invasion with *Pussycat in Memory of Darkness*.

Rediscoveries of neglected work – most commissioned by the Finborough Theatre – have included the first London revivals of Rolf Hochhuth's *Soldiers* and *The Representative*, both parts of Keith Dewhurst's *Lark Rise to Candleford*, *Etta Jenks* with Clarke Peters and Daniela Nardini, three rediscoveries from Noël Coward, and Lennox Robinson's *Drama at Inish* with Celia Imrie and Paul O'Grady. Transfers have included Emlyn Williams' *Accolade*, and John Van Druten's *London Wall* to St James' Theatre, and J. B. Priestley's *Cornelius* to a sell-out Off Broadway run in New York City.

Music Theatre has included the new (premieres from Craig Adams, Grant Olding, Charles Miller, Michael John LaChuisa, Adam Guettel, Andrew Lippa, Paul Scott Goodman, Polly Pen, and Adam Gwon's *Ordinary Days* which transferred to the West End) and the old (the UK premiere of Rodgers and Hammerstein's *State Fair* which also transferred to the West End), and the acclaimed 'Celebrating British Music Theatre' series.

The Finborough Theatre won the 2020 and 2022 London Pub Theatres Pub Theatre of the Year Award, *The Stage* Fringe Theatre of the Year Award in 2011, the Empty Space Peter Brook Award in 2010 and 2012, and was nominated for an Olivier Award in 2017 and 2019. Artistic Director Neil McPherson was awarded the Critics' Circle Special Award for Services to Theatre in 2019. It is the only unsubsidised theatre ever to be awarded the Channel 4 Playwrights Scheme bursary twelve times.

www.finboroughtheatre.co.uk

118 Finborough Road, London SW10 9ED
admin@finboroughtheatre.co.uk
www.finboroughtheatre.co.uk

The Finborough Theatre is a member of the Independent Theatre Council, the Society of Independent Theatres, Musical Theatre Network, The Friends of Brompton Cemetery, The Earl's Court Society, The Kensington Society, and supports #time4change's Mental Health Charter.

Supported by
The Theatres Trust Theatres Protection Fund Small Grants Programme, supported by The Linbury Trust
The Carne Trust
The Earls Court Development Company

The Finborough Theatre has the support of the Peggy Ramsay Foundation / Film 4 Playwrights Awards Scheme.

Mailing
Email admin@finboroughtheatre.co.uk or give your details to our Box Office staff to join our free email list.

Playscripts
Many of the Finborough Theatre's plays have been published and are on sale from our website.

Environment
The Finborough Theatre has a 100% sustainable electricity supply.

Local History
The Finborough Theatre's local history website is online at
www.earlscourtlocalhistory.co.uk

On Social Media
www.facebook.com/FinboroughTheatre
www.twitter.com/finborough
www.instagram.com/finboroughtheatre
www.youtube.com/user/finboroughtheatre
www.tiktok.com/@finboroughtheatre

Friends

The Finborough Theatre is a registered charity. We receive no public funding, and rely solely on the support of our audiences. Please do consider supporting us by becoming a member of our Friends of the Finborough Theatre scheme. There are four categories of Friends, each offering a wide range of benefits.

Richard Tauber Friends – David and Melanie Alpers. James Baer. Simon Bolland. Malcolm Cammack. James Carroll. Michael Coyle. Richard Dyer. Catrin Evans. Deirdre Feehan. Jeff Fergus. David Grier. Christine Hoenigs. Damien Hyland. Richard Jackson. Paul and Lindsay Kennedy. David Korman. Martin and Wendy Kramer. Georgina and Dale Lang. John Lawson. Emilia Leese. Rebecca Maltby. Kathryn McDowall. Ian Mitchell. Frederick Pyne. Maroussia Richardson. L Schulz. Brian Smith. James Stitt. Kathleen and Patrick Street. Janet Swirski. Lavinia Webb. Joan Weingarten and Bob Donnalley. John Wilkes. Steven Williams. Laura Winningham. Sylvia Young.

William Terriss Friends – Anonymous. Patrick Foster. Janet and Leo Liebster. Ros and Alan Haigh.

Adelaide Neilson Friends – Charles Glanville. Philip G Hooker.

Legacy Gifts – Tom Erhardt.

The Return of Benjamin Lay

Naomi Wallace's plays have been produced in the United Kingdom, the United States, Europe and the Middle East and include *One Flea Spare, The Trestle at Pope Lick Creek, In the Heart of America, Slaughter City, Things of Dry Hours, The Fever Chart: Three Visions of the Middle East, And I and Silence, The Liquid Plain, Night is a Room* and an adaptation of *Returning to Haifa* by Ghassan Kanafani and *The Corpse Washer* by Sinan Antoon (both adaptations co-written with Ismail Khalidi). Wallace's awards include the MacArthur Award, Susan Smith Blackburn Prize, Fellowship of Southern Writers Drama Award, Horton Foote Award, Obie Award, Arts and Letters Award in Literature, and the inaugural Windham Campbell prize for drama. Wallace is currently writing the book for the new John Mellencamp musical *Small Town* and co-writing the book for the new Loretta Lynn musical with George C. Wolfe.

Marcus Rediker, writer and historian, is Distinguished Professor of Atlantic History at the University of Pittsburgh. His 'histories from below', including *The Slave Ship: A Human History*, have won numerous awards, including the George Washington Book Prize, and have been translated into eighteen languages worldwide. He is the author of *The Fearless Benjamin Lay: The Quaker Dwarf Who Became the First Revolutionary Abolitionist* (Verso), co-author (with David Lester and Paul Buhle) of *Prophet against Slavery: Benjamin Lay, A Graphic Novel* (Verso) and producer of a prize-winning documentary film, *Ghosts of Amistad*, directed by Tony Buba. He worked with Naomi Wallace on her play *The Liquid Plain*. He is currently writing a book about escaping slavery by sea in antebellum America.

also by Naomi Wallace from Faber

BIRDY
SLAUGHTER CITY
THE TRESTLE AT POPE LICK CREEK
THE INLAND SEA
THINGS OF DRY HOURS
AND I AND SILENCE
RETURNING TO HAIFA
(*with Ismail Khalidi, adapted from the novella by Ghassan Kanafani*)
THE BREACH

NAOMI WALLACE
and
MARCUS REDIKER

The Return of Benjamin Lay

faber

First published in 2023
by Faber and Faber Limited
The Bindery, 51 Hatton Garden
London, ECIN 8HN

Typeset by Brighton Gray
Printed and bound in the UK by CPI Group (Ltd), Croydon CRO 4YY

A CIP record for this book
is available from the British Library

ISBN 978-0-571-38729-8

2 4 6 8 10 9 7 5 3 1

The Return of Benjamin Lay was first performed at the Finborough Theatre, London, on 13 June 2023, with the following cast:

Benjamin Lay Mark Povinelli

Director Ron Daniels
Set Designers Riccardo Hernandez and Isobel Nicolson
Costume Designer Isobel Nicolson
Lighting Designer Anthony Doran
Sound Designer John Leonard
Movement Consultant Bill Irwin
Stage Manager Martha J. Baldwin
Producer Arsalan Sattari

To Benjamin, Sarah, Bussa,
and all those, remembered or forgotten,
who fought for an earthly paradise.

And to Shayne and Henry,
our brothers, always with us.

Character

Benjamin Lay
returning from the eighteenth century,
a dwarf and hunchback

Setting

*In a Quaker Meeting House,
in Benjamin's mind,
in our minds.
1730s and now.*

Time

Now and then.

Note on the Text

/ signals an interruption at the end of the word.

THE RETURN OF BENJAMIN LAY

The public is seated and the lights go down. When the lights come up, we find Benjamin Lay seated with the audience. From this silence, when the spirit moves him, he will stand and begin to speak. Ben is barefoot, dressed in simple, undyed, home-made clothes and hat. Everything about him hints at older times.

Benjamin I know I am not part of the order of your meeting. And I do apologize for what happened the last time I was here. But it is urgent I speak to you now and it cannot wait.

But I forget my manners. Greetings, dear Friends. Are you well? Are you happy? Good. I am glad. For I have come a long way and quickly it seems, quickly even though it was long, but God gives me strength and he's given me these minutes to speak.

Believe me, dear, beloved Friends, I am honored that you have allowed me into this finest of . . . Quaker meeting houses. May I continue?

He listens for an answer, then steps on stage.

Thank you. But first, may I gently remind you of your judgment against me? 'Benjamin Lay, you have caused great disorder in our meetings and transgressed our most cherished Quaker values. You have viciously attacked our leading members. You have kidnapped our children. We do cast you out like a leper and nevermore shall you be allowed to participate in the meetings of the Society of Friends.'

I am no kidnapper and I am no leper.

Benjamin unbuttons the top of his shirt to show his chest.

As you can see, I have not a single leprous canker on my body! I am as pure as a newborn lamb and I have come here this hour to tell you that I am worthy to be your Brother again.

He pats down his clothes and begins to empty a little dirt from his pockets. Perhaps he finds a beetle there?

Are you familiar with beetles? Living jewels, they are. Not pests to me but sparks of divinity! Captivating as any creature on God's earth. The Dung Beetle, the Ox Beetle, the Giant Stag Beetle. If only Dürer had engraved the Rhinoceros Beetle instead of the animal itself, for its second horn is true. But when Dürer drew the animal, he had never actually seen the Rhinoceros with his own eyes. He imagined it from the words of others. He looked through those words and his pencil drew, but did he *see*?

But beetles, alas, are not what I want to speak to you about. No. No.

He begins again.

As a youth in Essex I tended them in the fields of old England. Not beetles, sheep. Do you have any idea how many I've counted in all these years and still no sleep? So quiet these animals, as quiet as stones but woolly like clouds and they make a sound not like clouds but like this:

He bleats like a lamb. It's not a good imitation.

That's not a lamb, is it? . . . That's a cloud! How a cloud sounds if you listen carefully, which I'd do walking here and there, always walking, subsisting on acorns and peaches, never burdening a horse to carry me. But lambs sound more like this.

He bleats like a lamb. Better.

Almost? Why don't you try the sound of a lamb?

He encourages an audience member to bleat.

And you. How is your bleat?

If it's not well done, Benjamin does it himself.

Like that, yes! Such a sound, it cannot but create in the most brutish hearts a quietening. A quickening quietening. A tendering. A teaching. As it does in me, brothers and sisters. But a sheep is not a rock nor a cloud. Nor am I the man you think I am. That you whisper and titter and scoff that I am. My name is Benjamin Lay, and I am a lamb, a cloud that's sheared so the rain'll come down like wool and keep you warm. Do you feel that kindness? That considerate weather? That is who I am. It is true I've done – (*Beat.*) extravagant things, every one of them a brutal trial in my soul, but all in service of God's Truth.

And yet, Friends, so often when I'd speak in our meetings about our sins, you'd cough, shuffle your feet, make noises to distract from my message.

You'd laugh at me, mock my body.

Yes. This body. Right here. Please, go ahead. Take a good hard look.

He unbuttons his shirt further or even takes it off.

Do you see? I give you permission. Stare! Glare! My hands? My feet? My ears? What are the first words in your head? Little Man? Tiny Man? What's that I hear? Runt? A grunting runt? Nice rhyme that one. Or . . . let's be a little more truthful: a mouthy midget, eh? A pint-sized pig? There! There! Do you feel that tingling in your own shape as your bodies stretch and sit up taller, ever so grateful *not to be like me*?

(*He speaks quickly, playfully.*) *Anything he can do I can do better?* Well. We shall see, because seeing is not the same as looking. You are looking at me now, but do you *see*?

15

What does the Lamb say? The lamb says, if I may be so bold, this lamb says: Banish me not from your flock. Though I stink, though I rot, though I rend, I am whole only when I am one among the many and the many is you. I am far from my flock and I am cold like a rock, far like a cloud. I've been lost without you and I want to come home. Will you let me come home?

Benjamin looks closely at his audience.

Our time is short, my love for the Quaker meeting is long and the fellowship, the blessed silence as we commune together, the gathering of spirits, intimations of the soul about our purposes here on earth, all in sweet unity, pure, peaceable, precious /

He cuts himself off. He looks up mischievously.

I have walked on water. Yes! No, I do not blaspheme. Walked on water like the Whirligig or Water Penny. I was a sailor! And once you become a sailor, you become . . . an amphibian!

Benjamin now walks sailor-style, swinging his body from side to side in rhythm with the waves. He now has his sea-legs.

And oh how the flesh transforms on that water, the body roiling in its liquid up and down, back and forth until you're as weightless as air.

Using his sailor's walk modified to suggest the sailing of a ship, Benjamin walks/sails a map of the Atlantic.

Where? The Mediterranean, over to the Caribbean, up and down the North American coast, all 'round the Atlantic. Our magnificent engine of canvas, wood and hemp, gliding 'cross those blue water empires. And while I climbed aloft to work the sails, below me the Captain, the little King of our wooden factory, bawled his commands 'gainst the wind as it whistled through the rigging. In stormy seas the timbers groaned as we cursed the waves. We cursed the Captain too, when we were downwind of him.

Benjamin stops a moment, considering the audience.

What's that? What did you say? Nothing? Oh but I can hear you thinking: Who'd hire a dwarf, a cripple, a Jack Sprat like *him* to man a ship? How could such a misshapen thing work the capstan or hoist the sails?!

He is suddenly calm again.

Misshapen. I learned that word as a child before 'water' or 'bread'. It rustled above my cradle.

Ignorance, my Friends, is the second cousin of the nephew's niece to the devil's brother. You see, you . . . landlubbing hayseed country clowns don't know the ways of a ship. But I do! I was quick as a mouse up and down the rigging, untangling and tying knots where my fellow tars couldn't reach. I'd hang on the sails and mend them without ever tearing the canvas.

Look at that picture in your mind, Friends. The wee man dangling by his little arms from the sails as his tiny hands make quick repairs. Look, look! But do you *see*? Yes, I dangled but I never fell. Could you scurry across the yard-arm while sharks wait beneath you with open jaws? Hmmm?

Kinfolk, will you hear me? A King once listened to me, though I'm not sure he *heard*. I was naught but a common sailor in my slops but I spoke straight at him, for that is who I am. Would *you* argue with a King?

King George II it was. Bustle, bustle, went the retinue all around the King – silk and servants galore.

Benjamin becomes the King. The King shows himself off to the audience. The King is playful but dangerous.

The King I am the King. I bustle, I swing and you sing. My staff and my throne are emblazoned with gold –

Benjamin – mined by the dead in Brazil, in Africa –

The King – and my cape swarms with a hundred animals that still blink when I caress them, sewn with a thousand silk threads –

Benjamin – made by the tiniest, fine-iest hands in India –

The King – Oh India!

The King now notices Benjamin waiting for him.

Greetings, my good subject, my tiniest of subjects –

Benjamin (*as himself*) Greetings, George. My name is Benjamin Lay. I am here to /

The King cuts him off.

The King I am 'Your Majesty'. Mind your mouth or I shall pluck out your tongue.

Benjamin No offense, George, but I'm here /

The King I know why you're here. A king always knows! It's your day of good fortune. I will take you on.

Benjamin You will take me /

The King calls to someone.

The King Tailor, come get this little man's measurements!

The King calls to Jeffrey.

Little Jeffrey! Little Jeffrey?! You rapscallion, are you hiding? He's always hiding! Nitwit, come out or we'll hang you by your feet again!

The King 'watches' as a dwarf, Little Jeffrey, appears.

(*To Little Jeffrey.*) Ah Jeffrey, come meet your fellow courtier. You will have a playmate just as small as you – and you can run and hide and snicker together in the tiniest, darkest hidey-holes in the court.

The King is disturbed that Benjamin is laughing.

How dare you laugh, Commoner Lay! It's not your place to laugh at Little Jeffrey. Only the King laughs at his jester. Only the King laughs at all. Stop. Stop laughing or my guards will make you stop! Isn't this why you came?

Benjamin No.

The King To be a court jester?

Benjamin Uh, no.

The King I will decide if you'll be my court jester! If you resist I'll peg your head to the wall like the deer I hunt!

Benjamin George, I have brought you a gift.

The King A gift? I like gifts. Does it wind up? Does it pop out? Does it tickle one's tethers?

Benjamin I brought you a / book.

The King (*disappointed*) A book. Hmmm. You've brought me a book. Blah, blah . . . What book? Hmmm. Fairy tales?

Benjamin Not quite.

The King Dragon tales?

Benjamin Not exactly.

The King Tiny men with tiny hands tales?

Benjamin Certainly not.

The King inspects the book.

The King (*disappointed*) A volume by John Milton. Hmm. Did we not behead this regicide?

Benjamin No. He /

The King Not hanged?

Benjamin No.

The King Drawn?

Benjamin No.

The King Quartered?

Benjamin No. He survived to write /

The King *Considerations touching the Likeliest Means to Remove Hirelings out of the Church.* Summarize the book. One line only.

Benjamin Milton and I humbly ask your Kingly self and the Queen's Queenly self to see what a pack of destructive vermin you have preaching in the Church of England.

The King Did you say 'vermin'? In my Church? I am the 'Supreme Governor of the Church of England' and I have no vermin /

Benjamin (*in one breath*) I would say 'rats', George. But rats are a nobler species because they fatten on cheese while your Church of England vermin suck the marrow of the poor. Being equal in the eyes of God has as much meaning to them as . . .

(*To the audience.*) I didn't finish because the King raised his finger. Just one finger, as if testing the air.

    The King raises his finger.

Next thing I knew I awoke in a stinking cell, upside down, hanging from my feet, a bloody knot on my head. But I did not cry out, Brothers and Sisters. No, I sang, head over heels with joy, because I knew the King would not be able to put the poet back in the bag and Milton's words would swarm like bees about the high ceilings and the King's face so red with the stings. (*Beat.*) That is the kind of man I am: *A man who fears God fears not men in high degree.* Fellow Quakers, I defended our Godly people against the King and his wicked, venal Church. I did it for Truth. I did it for you . . .

    Benjamin selects people in the audience.

. . . and you and also you.

So I ask you now in turn: Will you take me back into the fold? Your fold. Undo the disown of me and disown the undo of me because . . . I love you.

It is a warm autumn day the first time I sit as a child in a Quaker meeting. The floorboards sweat their woody perfume beneath our feet. The sheared wool on the benches cushions our seat. We sit in shared silence of worship, all on a level. Only when a brother or sister stands to speak from the Inward Light is the quiet interrupted. And then silence again, bodies still and peaceful. And as I sit in that silence like an empty jug, the essence of God pours down into me and fills me up and I know I am as pure a vessel of God's love as anyone in the room, that God does not *look* at my body, He *sees* it. Sees it! And that seeing makes us one in the eyes of our Lord.

I miss the meditation that engulfs us, peels away our worldly goods and dissolves us until we are without Noise of Words, suspended between the living and dead where God breathes on us – and we breathe back. I miss that community of souls. So I beg of thee, Friends, let me join you once again. I am harmless. Harmless as a lost lamb . . . Well, almost, for who among us does not carry a stanza of Milton in a secret pocket of skin like something alive and ready to pop? Just like this . . .

Benjamin produces a book.

This. What is this? My book, *All Slave-Keepers that Keep the Innocent in Bondage, Apostates.* Yes, I wrote it. How, you might wonder, does a man with so little education come to do such a thing? Well, it came from the sea. Just like me. Written by these hands, hardened by pulling rope.

Benjamin opens the book and reads from it with an exaggerated sense of purpose.

'*Written for a General Service, by him that truly and sincerely desires the present and eternal Welfare and Happiness of all Mankind, all the World over, of all Colors, and Nations, as his own Soul.*'

He snaps shut the book.

His own soul. *The* soul. *Our* soul.

I could have been a farmer like my father or a shepherd all my life, for I was in line to inherit the family farm in Copford.

As I sat with my back to the trunk of a giant Oak, the grass beneath me began to sway, the branches whispered like waves, and the wind came up sharp. I looked out over the green hills and I wondered, what learning lay beyond the rock and cloud and sheep? That wonder swept me from our Copford farm onto the docks of London! Where I signed on a ship! A ship would be my school!

His body begins to sway as he mimics the motion of the ocean. He is off-center but never mind, he continues with glee.

Some sailors carried books in their sea chests and these men I pestered with questions till one knocked me down. But I got up and kept on a-asking. Why? Because I had a hole inside me where the shape of nothing would fit. And that hole, dear Friends, was that I could not. Read. But a messmate took a shine to me. Daniel Baker, an old salt, taught me my letters.

Benjamin hunkers down to suggest the cramped, intimate quarters of the foc'sle where Baker taught him to read. He reads with difficulty.

'. . . being in a ship is being in a jail, with the chance of being drowned . . . a man in a jail has more room, better food, and commonly better company.'

(*Calling out triumphantly.*) 'A man in jail has more room, better food, and commonly better company!'

But a ship was no jail to me! I prize the ocean, vast and deep and full of God's wonders.

And not once but many a time on that ocean I faced down the dangers of King Death.

You see, it was common for a tar to be afflicted by the black gums of scurvy and when his teeth fell out, he'd carry them in his pocket, rattle them to a tune. Others died from sickness we'd never seen, their skin transparent as water and through it you'd see their hearts stop. Oftentimes in a storm a shipmate was swept overboard into merciless seas, his cries marked by gulls until he went deep under. Did I grieve for my dead fellow tars? Aye. All of us did, and we never forgot them: Black Bill Davidson, Timmy O'Toole, Minus Jones.

Though the men who owned the ships and grew rich from the trade never knew those names. Do you? Not just those tars on the sea but those commoners, men and women both, you have paid or used or punished to do your labor and give you gain?

Back to his sea story –

Ah. But there's water, water everywhere, and after only three voyages, I'm assigned to the foretop, high above the main deck, mine eyes feasting on the ocean and its majestic roll for miles in every direction. The glory of God's seascape is that there is no dominating it: It dominates you.

On our watch aloft we'd have a Dutchman, a Greek, an Irishman and an African. We were as motley as Little Jeffrey's garment! One hand for the ship and one hand for yourself, that was our motto, but in truth we tars always had hands for each other. And yes, in all ways, 'hands for each other'.

(*Aside, to an audience member.*) Sometimes one tar'd pop his brother's sail and the other'd pop his. Helping hands, eh?

23

(*Back to everyone.*) But mostly our hands kept us alive, dividing the work, sharing our wages when we went ashore. On ships I learned there is no such thing as me or you, only and always 'us'. Alone against the elements, we die. Our only hope is 'one and all', a sailor's shout if ever there was one.

Benjamin begins to sing with energy.

'*Oh the times was hard and the wages low*
  Leave her, Johnny, leave her
And the grub was bad and the gales did blow
  And it's time for us to leave her.'

Twelve years at sea, half my fellow tars crippled or dead, I was pushing my luck. But *leave her*? No. To find her. And that is what I did.

One Sarah Smith, working gal in Deptford –

He whistles long and with appreciation.

– sensuous, vigorous, curious. Not like a Butterfly or a Glow Worm, bah, too easy. More like a . . . Candy-Striped Leafhopper! Beautiful, tiny, quick.

Where do I find such a sparkler? Docked on the Thames, I desert my ship on a First Day morning so I can go to a Quaker meeting. The master of the press-gang will never look for a runaway sailor in a house of worship!

I see her sitting in the women's gallery of the Deptford Monthly. She looks right past my salt-stained frock, my tarred baggy breeches and *sees* me. I can tell by the curl of her eyes and the shine of her lips that she fancies this sailor. She is not the first to curl and shine for me. A bit of a lady's man I was as a lad. You see, tall women fancied me too, for I knew how to /

Benjamin cuts himself off.

But Sarah! She is my own size and a perfect match. Truth is, she's a little smaller than me but she is my equal. And as ready as flint! The first time . . . Do you remember the first time you kissed a mouth you loved?

Our first kiss hits me like a rogue wave I never saw coming. My heart races as I'm thrown into the spray, thinking I might die right then and there – and a lucky man I'd be if I did!

Do you remember the kind of kiss that cuts you off at the ankles?

He approaches the audience.

Have you ever had such a kiss? Don't be shy. How about you? Yes? Good. And you? And you?

Benjamin finds an audience member who is unsure.

That's too bad, for such a kiss can make you dance an Irish jig!

Benjamin very briefly dances, then cuts his reverie off.

Well, let's just say I knew it was time to leave the sea.

My friend Bussa would later say when he saw Sarah and me together, 'That little buckra man' – that's a white man to all of you – 'he go all over the world to find that little buckra woman for himself.' Truth is, I didn't have to go very far. We married the next year and soon sailed to Barbados. Too much strife in England. Too many rich ones, vain, leech-like, oppressing their fellow /

He cuts himself off.

Do you know the Herring Gull? These sea birds live near the water but they fly inland to swoop down on a lamb and pluck out its tongue. So tasty for the Herring Gull, like a wriggling pink fish. But without its tongue the lamb can no longer suckle. It dies.

Benjamin glances around the room.

Do I see one or two Herring Gulls in this very room? I just might know for I have fought some of you off /

*Benjamin is suddenly a somber, pompous, 'weighty
Quaker', John Kinsey.*

John Kinsey Benjamin Lay! We do cast you out of the
Quaker meeting!

Benjamin (*to the audience*) John Kinsey, Clerk of the
Quaker Meeting and Chief Justice of the Supreme Court,
represents all that is wrong in the world.

(*To Kinsey, in a prophetic voice.*) The Great Red Dragon's
tail gathered up a third of the stars of heaven and cast them
to the earth. And there was war in heaven: Michael and his
angels fought against the dragon and cast him out.

(*To the audience again.*) Woe to the inhabiters of the earth
and of the sea! For the Devil is come down unto you. Those
stars flung down to earth sprouted slave-keepers, the spawn
of Satan.

John Kinsey Your evil book, *All Slave-Keepers*, abuses our
leading members and the whole Society of Friends!

*Benjamin looks at Kinsey, then stares at the audience,
saying nothing.*

You sow division amongst us! We cast you out of the
Quaker meeting! Out! Out!

Benjamin Out! Cast out by the Great Red Dragon himself!
But ah-ha! I still have my tongue!

Do you still have yours? And what about you?

(*To an audience member.*) Stick out your tongue then. Yours
looks healthy enough. And what about your tongue, do you
still have it? Good. Because a tongue is for saying *No* when
a *No* is required /

Benjamin cuts himself off.

I had to say *No*. I just couldn't do it so my older brother
would. When a lamb lost its tongue, a rock was required.

Crack, crack went the rock on their skulls. What did it matter? Sheep are stupid creatures.

But it's not true at all! That's why I love them. Intelligent, sheep are, and mine were, and I had the kenning. In my small flock I knew each one from the other by its ears, marks and walk-about. Our sheep, for generations, had a stroke mark down the shoulder and a pop on the near uggon. That's how others knew they were ours on the commons.

And when one of the lambs died, the mother would pine, and if she made up her mind to die, she would die. So we'd cut the skin off the dead one, slice free 'round the ankles, front, back and neck, and pull the skin off in one piece. Then we'd take a lamb from another ewe who had three, three being too many to nurse, and fit it with the skin of the dead lamb, tight as a sweater. And the pining mother would think her lamb had returned from the grave and she'd get up off her knees and she'd suckle it.

I too have returned from the dead. Take me in. Suckle me. The skin I wear to give me shape does not make me an imposter. For under this skin I am you and you are me and the sheep and the cloud and the world. You once believed this: That all of us are one and the same till death do us part.

He looks hard at the audience.

'Till death do us part'! Sarah and I swore those same words to one another before we sailed to to Barbados. Ah, Barbados! A small island but a rich one. The crown jewel in the British imperial tiara. So Sarah and I joined the Quakers in Bridgetown and set up shop on the waterfront. We rented two rooms of a warehouse on a bustling wharf. Slept above, sold below. Stocked our little shop with simple, useful things. Candles, flour, paper and knives. Didn't like selling rum, but I knew sailors.

We traded with the lads who came and went on the vessels. With craftsmen who buzzed about the ships like flies and screeching women fishmongers. Mostly we got enslaved people coming to our store, especially on First Day when they came to market in town. That is how I met Bussa. He was an Igbo man and a cooper three times my size.

Bussa helps me unload boxes from a ship arrived in Bridgetown. A few things for the shop. Loud voices churn, haggle, laugh and curse in a dozen different languages. Bussa stops, puts down his load, and lustily breathes in the chaos. He says with a crooked smile, 'God hath made of one blood all nations to dwell on the face of the earth.' I am so startled I drop the box I'm carrying. I cannot answer. Bussa had memorized Acts 17:26. The evidence is all around us, for everyone to see. We are of one blood! One and all. We keep working, Bussa and I, but in that moment I know I've found a friend of my soul.

Bussa was handsome, oh yes, even Sarah said so. Smartest man I met there. Though it's hard to be smart when you're hungry. Bussa had a way of saying my name, Ben-jahhh-meen, taking his time, as though it had never been said before. Even when he hadn't eaten for days he was sharp as a shark's tooth and shrewd as a frigate bird.

And Bussa had hands as large as . . . large as pineapples?

I met other noble fruits on Barbados – plantains, bananas and papayas – and my favorite, the pin-pillow pear. Thanks to God's presence in all living things, these innocent fruits grow with no human or animal oppression. Life in harmony with nature, saith old Diogenes. Now sugar is a different story. A story of nightmares! The trade in sugar is /

Cuts himself off again.

In my last years alive I lived in a cave. 'A cave?! A cave?!' Fools laugh but holy people have lived in caves since the time of Jeremiah the prophet. Though I'm not saying I'm holy. I wouldn't dare say that. I would do my best not even to think it. Only that . . . well, the quiet is good for the soul and it reminded me of the tranquility I'd lost with you.

Friends and neighbors came to visit. I'd receive them politely and cover the table with my apples, peaches, walnuts, squash, radishes, potatoes and, my favorite, the humble turnip, covered in a lucent honey from my hard-working bees. Heavenly! The rich came too, to converse and observe my way of living. Governor Richard Penn, Ben Franklin.

I visited Franklin once in his home.

Benjamin puts on spectacles and becomes Ben Franklin. Franklin has a Boston accent and a kite. A storm is gathering.

Ben Franklin Welcome to my humble abode, Benjamin Lay.

Benjamin looks around. He is amused.

Benjamin Humble, did you say? Not as fancy as some of the rich Quakers, I'll grant you that. Why the kite?

Ben Franklin It's part of a new experiment! In these enlightened times, we have much to discuss.

Benjamin I accepted your invitation to visit because you kindly published my book. But why did you leave your printer's name off the title page?

Ben Franklin Did I leave off my name?

Benjamin Completely.

Ben Franklin Surely an oversight. I don't recall /

Benjamin (*interrupts*) I do. I have the book right here. Perhaps you didn't want Kinsey to see our names side by side –

Ben Franklin Nonsense.

Benjamin – like two old friends . . . who oppose human / bondage

Ben Franklin Let me tell you about the experiment /

Benjamin You've never spoken out against slavery in public. Why is that?!

Ben Franklin is silent.

Benjamin Franklin, dost thou keep slaves in thy household?

Ben Franklin No man can be perfect in his conduct, surely / you

Benjamin Your thoughts electrify us. You can power the Inward Light of divinity in all of us. But not if you enslave /

Ben Franklin Freedoms are incremental, Ben. Surely you /

Benjamin It is a crime against the moral order of creation! I refuse to partake of thy unrighteousness. I leave you, Ben Franklin, to your darkness!

(*As himself again.*) . . . and go back to my cave.

In my cave I had a wooden bowl and a hammock, simple habits from my sailing days. And my tools: axe, adze, hammer and hoe. And spinning. Ah, that sound like water rushing. Skeins of flax, I spun on my spindle and wove them into my own clothes – tow linen. No animal skins for me. No violence of any kind permitted, not even shearing.

I lived outside the market place. I grew my own food. I lived not on the labor of others, not even when it was hidden in 'goods' – why do they call them 'goods' when they conceal the sweat and blood of those who make them? I consumed nothing made by slave labor. A little money I had, but I'd no need for it.

(*Whispering, as though sharing a secret.*) Except to buy books. They were my land of milk and honey.

(*Erupting with delight.*) The King James Bible, of course. History, poetry, theology, philosophy! What do you have on your shelves, brothers and sisters? You? What books are you reading? What would you recommend?

He gets some titles from his audience.

Ah . . . I must read those!

In my cave I had two hundred books of all kinds and sizes: folio, quarto, octavo, twelves! I lent them out to anyone who'd read them. Sometimes I'd even dream of my books and I'd wake in the dark with a thirst to read again a line or two by Leo Africanus, bright genius of the continent, or Sandiford's *Mystery of Iniquity*. Poor Ralph, driven to madness by Kinsey's persecution /

Benjamin breaks off, then he's right away into the next section.

And on my desk, the best collection in all of Pennsylvania on our glorious Quaker founders! George Fox, James Nayler, Margaret Fell. They did extravagant things too, let us not forget!

(*Quietly, confiding.*) Well, maybe they didn't smash the finest china with a hammer to show that tea-drinking kills those who harvest tea and sugar. And yes, I once hid a young boy in my cave – I did not kidnap him! When his mother and father grew hysterical, I returned the boy. Only then did they learn how the African parents felt when the young girl they hold in bondage was stolen.

I have all the founders! And Edward Burrough, one of my favorites: 'You may destroy these vessels . . . yet our principles you can never extinguish, but they will live for ever, and enter into other bodies to live and speak and act.' So he said to the rich men of Parliament as they brought the vermin, King Charles II, back to the throne. Thank goodness he was the last King Charles. But vermin come in packs. They /

He cuts himself off.

Once in a rage I killed a ground-hog that visited my cave. The animal had eaten the turnips in my garden. I quartered its body and hung the bloody parts on a stick at each corner as a terror to the others. I awoke in the middle of the night, tormented by my own cruelty. By candlelight I collected the pieces of the ground-hog and vainly tried to put the poor varmint back together.

That hungry fellow creature had as much right to the turnips as I did. Why should I murder a being full of life? Why should we kill and eat our . . . neighbors? I got down on my knees to bury the severed body and vowed to the heavens that I would never kill another animal nor eat its flesh.

Benjamin's guilt moves him to cursing as Queen Margaret –

Queen Margaret
'Thou slander of thy mother's heavy womb!
Thou loathed issue of thy father's loins!
Thou rag of honor! Thou detested –'

Benjamin quiets himself.

Benjamin We'll never know, will we, what Queen Margaret was going to say after 'Thou detested –'? Before she was rudely cut off by the Duke of Gloucester. What do you think she might have said? *Thou rag of honor! Thou detested* . . . What?

Well, my fellow sailors and I, we chewed on that question when we stepped into the Bard of Avon's comedies and tragedies in the slack hours aboard our ship. When we conjured up those words, we'd spin to Cyprus to Florence to Rome and back to Windsor, all at the flap of a sail.

But I told my mates: No. I will not. I refuse. No, no, no . . . No! I don't care if I was perfectly made to play King Richard III. And besides, he was taller than I am. Twins, hah? Just because we both have hunchbacks doesn't mean we're kinfolk . . . I do appreciate that you want me to have the leading part but I prefer to play . . . Queen Margaret! Quiet! Quiet down, Friends. I will play Queen Margaret or

I will play no one. How do you know Queen Margaret didn't have a hunchback? Huh? Did anyone ever ask her what she had hidden beneath her robes? Well then. It remains a mystery. I rest my case.

Queen Margaret *Foul wrinkled witch* am I? Yes, I was *banished on pain of death* . . . You banished me, Richard, because I speak the truth.

> '*Oh the sorrow that I have, by right is yours;*
> *And all the pleasures you usurp are mine.*'

Queen Margaret is silent some moments.

'*Thou elvish-marked, abortive, rooting hog!*'

Benjamin Oh was ever a curse more delicious in the mouth? Margaret, say it again!

Queen Margaret
'*Thou elvish-marked, abortive, rooting hog!*'

Suddenly Queen Margaret turns on Benjamin.

You there!

Benjamin Me?

Queen Margaret Yes, you, Commoner Lay! Standing in my Richard's shadow with your homunculus hunching of bone . . .

Benjamin Now, Margaret, there's no need to /

Queen Margaret (*interrupts*) It's 'Your Majesty' to you, you troll. You say you are one of us?

Benjamin Well, I /

Queen Margaret How dare you?! How dare you challenge us, accuse us of breaking God's laws? A Quaker like us? You? Ha! You are nothing but a puny, stunted crookback . . . *Thou rag of honor! Thou detested . . . Thou detested . . . Benjamin Lay!* We cast you out! Out.

Benjamin (*quietly*) Out again. I was thrown out of meeting after meeting in town after town. Nothing can wipe up the smear of that wound. Not even a visit from the Star-Nosed Mole who came to investigate what remained of me in my grave. What I saw in Barbados, even the worms and beetles and maggots could not turn to dust . . .

A dark shadow of horror remains with me, even though I am dissolved.

As a man of the world I thought I'd clapped my eyes on everything under the sun. But nothing like this . . .

Benjamin sees the vision in front of him again, but he reports it like facts:

A few climb into empty sugar barrels on the docks to die. I have seen them do it. But for their spirits, the enslaved would all die of hard labor, sickness, hunger. Ribs astir, they stagger into our shop by the hundreds on First Day after meeting. Their need is great and our means small but Sarah and I feed them in our home. One hand for yourself, the other for the crew.

Because of this, the great men send a rabble of poor buckra to throw stones through our window, pull down our shelves to frighten us.

Bussa had helped me build those shelves. As we stood measuring and hammering, he whispered news he'd heard on the docks: the slaves had risen on a plantation in St Philip's parish. 'Was anyone killed?' I asked. 'Yes,' Bussa answered, 'two or three.' He paused, then added, 'But buckra's killing is long and many, many more.' We worked on in silence. I thought to myself, God has come to take vengeance.

Two weeks later, north of the docks, Sarah and I visit Quaker Friends. As we approach their house at dusk, we see dangling below the branches of a big silk cotton tree a dark, trembling mass. As we draw near we see a man stripped naked, his arms pinned behind his back, hanging from a chain 'round his ribs. It is Bussa. His face is resolute but his body shivers. Blood pools on the ground beneath him. He looks at us but he does not speak, he does not ask our help. Then he turns his head away.

When we enter the Friends' house and ask why, they answer without sorrow: 'An overseer heard him tell the other slaves of an uprising in the eastern part of the island. He must be taught a lesson.' We beg for our friend. We barter. We berate. But they are heartless.

Later, two men dressed in silk, velvet and gold, darken the doorway of our shop. They call us misshapen Quaker dogs, accuse us of stirring up the Negros to violence and threatening His Majesty's most valuable colony. They banish us from the Island.

Sisters and brothers, do you know what sugar is? . . . Sugar is . . . In the tea it makes a little heaven for the tongue. If you still have a tongue. Some of the slaves, they didn't. The truth is, sugar is made of blood. D'ye know it? Blood. Come nearer to this nectar.

I do, when in my mind I walk again in the dark Satanic sugar mill and see with mine own eyes the boiling vats full of grease, dung, dirt and other filth, even the limbs of the enslaved that get caught in the machinery. Drink thy sweetened tea, dear cannibals!

With every cup of tea, you sip the life juice of tea-workers in India and sugar-workers in Barbados. You fill the fat, lazy bellies of slave-keepers who enclose and destroy the land, once the common treasury of all. Beware rich men who poison the earth for gain!

Sarah and I are forced to leave the Island. Before we sail, I go to see Bussa who is now locked in a cage in the center of town. I think: His hands are not like pineapples . . . What

35

a ridiculous thing to think, even to say. Bussa tells me he will be whipped again, in public, 'to keep me in awe'.

I'll bear it no longer, he says.

As we board our vessel, our friends line the docks, singing lamentations. Shall I ever forget them? Should we have stayed and done God's work against those horrors? Maybe. Most certainly. But Sarah and I could no longer breathe in the smoky darkness of ill-got wealth. Ill-got, yes. And everything piled on top of it ill-got as well. Dear Bussa, such courage amid the carnage. You chewed the seeds of the crab-eye vine and died that same day. No more beatings, no more profits for buckra man. You were a man of the Truth.

When we sail up the Delaware River toward our new home, Philadelphia, I can smell the slave ship before I see it. We watch our fellow creatures auctioned to the highest bidders in the square at Front and Market Streets.

A Quaker owns the ship and another runs the auction.

For the first time, he erupts in anger –

In Pennsylvania! In Penn's woods! Place of the Holy Experiment, where Quakers would begin the world anew. Liberty, tolerance, peace! Are these not the words you cherish? Equality! Sanctuary for all mankind! Ha!

He calms again.

William Penn. Do you honor him? Our founder owned twelve slaves! But surely he's the exception? He is no exception! He is like the rest of you, Quaker elders, leading ministers, clerks of our meetings, all sweet in the mouth as you justify the oppression of our fellow creatures! Greed, avarice, covetousness. Vanity and corruption. You built Babylon and I will tear it down.

My cave prepared me for the grave, but I can't say Sarah liked it much. We were living there when she fell ill of a fever. Sometimes I think the fever that ravaged her small frame came from living too close to the heat of my . . . conviction. Hers was a good passing – calm, confident in her faith. I've not been confident in mine since she left me. I've still a cave-full of doubt about my protests, my vexations that have lived in me since I was a boy. I asked her at the end, 'Why, dear Sarah, am I a man of such strife and contention? Why can't I live by our Quaker ideal of harmony?' She said to me, 'Your anger is good-hearted, Ben. But it's not sustenance.'

Sarah. *You* were my sustenance. If I could kiss you once more, I would rest in that Promised Land.

Oh, I have prayed many times that God would find someone greater than myself to carry the Biblical prophecy of Jubilee: the end of all enslavement and oppression. The great leveling. But he has not answered. Am I worthy of the cause? I've no education, no learning but what little I've gathered with the help of my shipmates. I am a weak vessel, a 'bruised reed'.

Beloved Friends, what should I have done? What should I have said? Was I to turn my back on my ministry? I've been to jail for what I believe . . .

As Benjamin continues to speak, he puts on a simple, ageless military uniform. If he needs it, he'll ask a member of the audience to help him.

How many of you have gone to jail for conscience? Please let me see your hands. Hmmm. I don't see many hands. But Bussa's hands. What were his hands like? The enslaved, what their hands were like? (*Beat.*) Books? Yes, books! And together they made vast libraries. I wake in my grave still craving to read what is inside those books, what was there in those hands, so much to teach us, which I didn't read, which we'll never read. Their books. Their hands. Their freedom. Which they built in spite of us.

I speak Truth but you call me an enemy of the Quaker experiment in Pennsylvania. Enemy? Ha! Your spittle on my face honors me. Your persecution and ridicule are holy to me. They show me the path toward the Light!

You merchants are murderers. Your crafty art of buying and selling has killed thousands of people. For all I know, you have killed hundreds of thousands in your vast, bloody, iniquitous, cursed slave trade.

Benjamin now produces a sword and a book. He is 'ready'.

Brothers? Sisters? Bah! Your property is nothing but stolen labor. I've seen nations rise and fall, come and go and at the stinking, hateful, rotten core of it all? Money – the love of money, the love of profit – the destruction of nations! And with that money came Leviathan, building empires of gristle and bone! Oh, greed, a capital sin that makes one think: *I am better than the rest. I will be free while others die in dungeons!* These sins are mighty, mighty, almost almighty monsters.

(*In a prophetic voice.*) If I whet my glittering sword, and mine hand take hold on judgment, I will render vengeance to mine enemy, and will reward them that hate me.

Benjamin pulls his sword from the scabbard.

I too will bear it no longer! I will tell the Truth: *God will take vengeance against those who oppress their fellow creatures!*

Benjamin runs the sword through the book. 'Blood' splashes out and gushes down his arm. Benjamin looks hard at the audience for some moments, unmoving, accusing. The book still raised. The 'blood' still trickling. Then Benjamin lowers the book. He's quiet again, giving us the facts.

I've spattered my petition again, haven't I? And now my time with you is up.

I, Benjamin Lay, came here today to ask you, to beg you: *Let me rejoin the Quaker community.*

But no, dear Friends, no. I see it clearly now: You need to join me as much as I need to join you. I'm no good alone and neither are you.

As Benjamin speaks, he may accidentally swipe his face, leaving 'blood' on his cheek.

In your hearts you know the truth: I was here among you three hundred years ago . . . Had you chosen differently then – before slavery and greed breathed their venom so deeply into our souls – we would be living in another world now. It is not too late to purge these poisons.

Let us build Paradise, without the blood of war and commerce on our hands! Paradise is earth and soil and children shrieking in their deliverance and food enough for all, eating and breathing together. Fair work for a just wage and blankets when it's cold, pure water to drink, and tongues and kisses for everyone, shelter from snow and hail and gardens of delectables to keep us all, animal and human, bright and strong. I will breathe for you, Bussa said, and you will breathe for me, yes, yes, and our canvas of wood and hemp will sail with not one hand left behind. Paradise! Powered by the wind which is God's breath and our breath and the Dung Beetle's breath, all breathing and laboring as one magnificent common engine!

I am ready to join hands, to build this new Jerusalem with you right here, right now. We can't wait to save ourselves, to save our earth. So what will it be? What shall we do?

Come then. Join me. We can make the finest work of one another, loving and leveling all things, great and small.

Come stand with me. Let's talk.

If people don't join, he may take a person's arm and encourage them so that others follow.

Yes, that's right. Get up. Come down here. You. And you too. Let's have a good look at one another, and keep looking until we *see*. Keep listening until we *hear*.

Friends, what dost thou say?

Better yet, what canst we do?

> *Benjamin begins to talk with those who have joined him on stage.*
>
> *The End.*